Map It!

Sharon Coan, M.S.Ed.

This is a **map**.

NORTH
ATLANTIC
OCEAN
RUSSIA
ATLANTIC
OCEAN

A map shows a **place**.

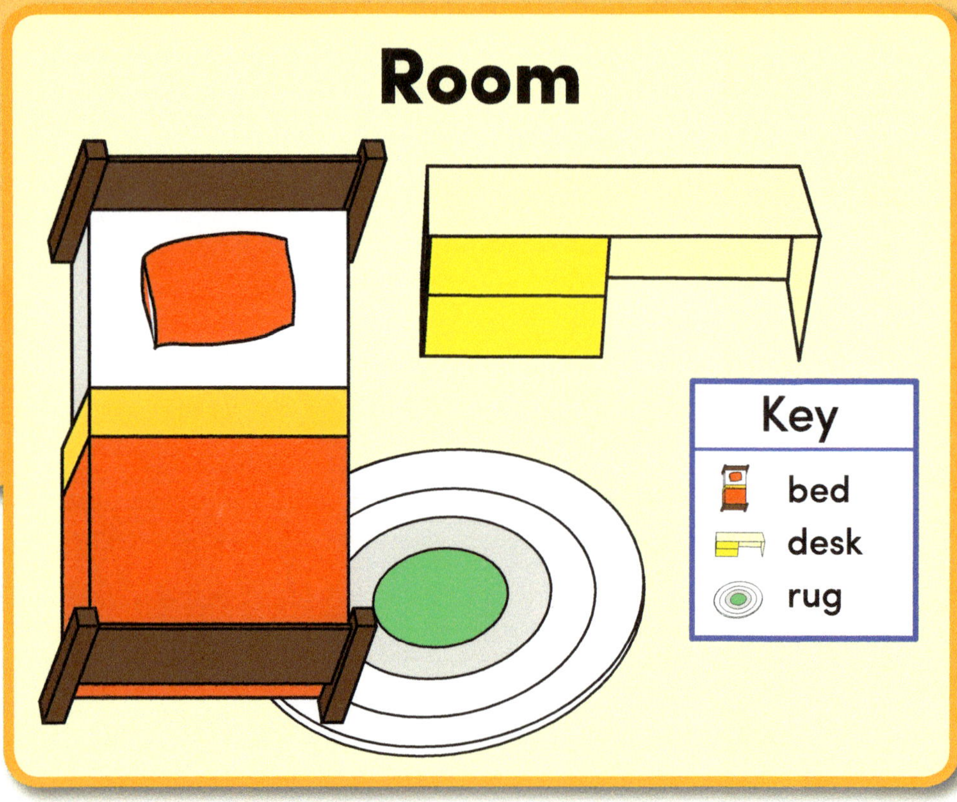

map

place

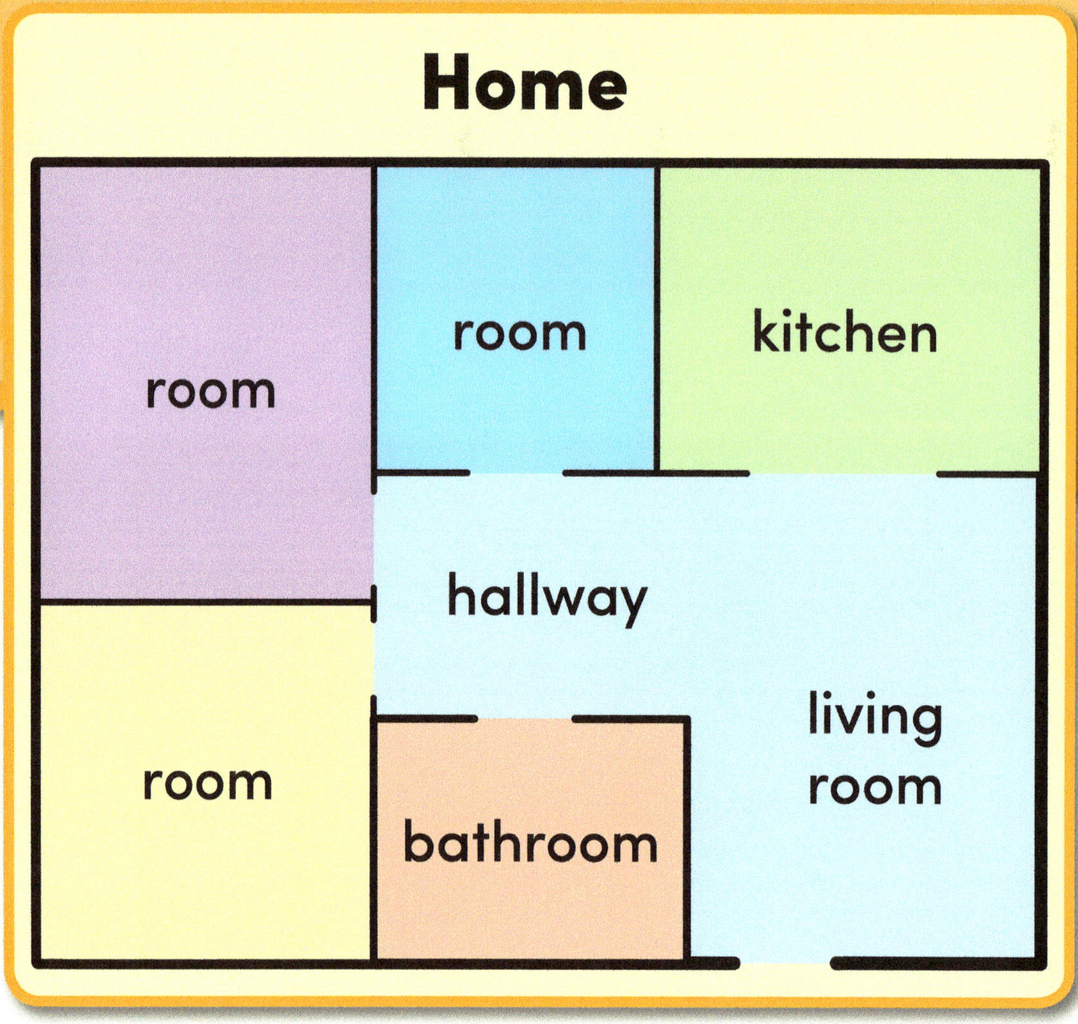

map

place

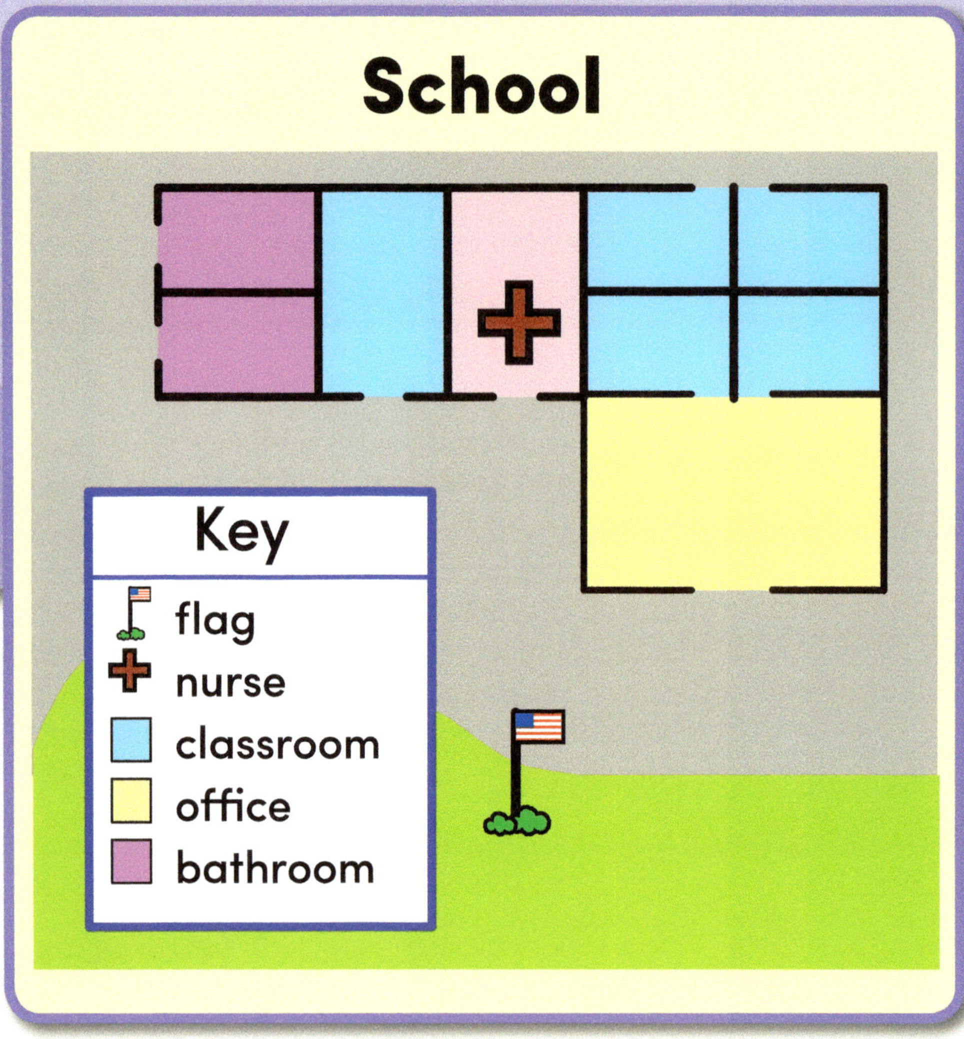

map

place

map

place

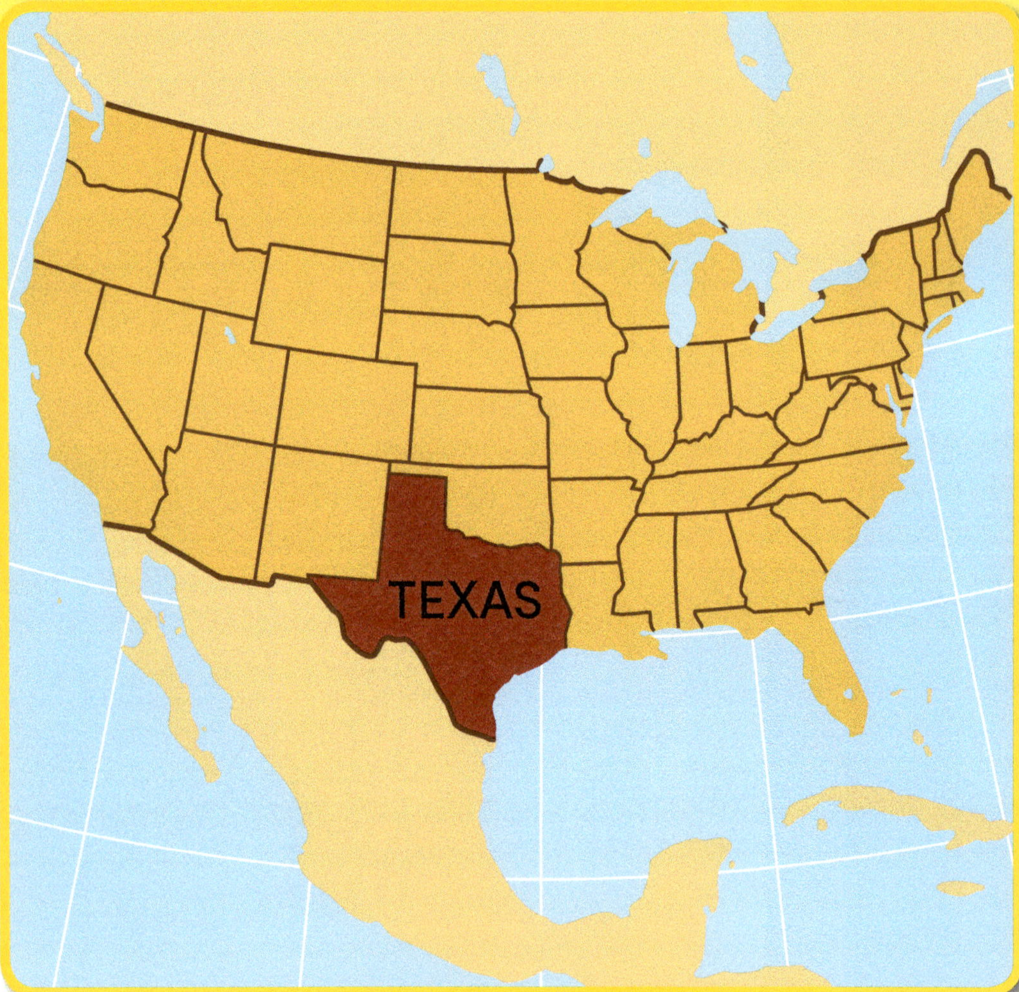

map

place

map

place

Draw It!

1. Choose a place.
2. Draw a map.

3. Tell about your map.

Glossary

map—a picture that shows a place

place—a part of the world

Index

Your Turn!

Have you ever seen a map? Where was it? Tell a friend.

Consultants

Shelley Scudder
Gifted Teacher
Broward County Schools

Caryn Williams, M.S.Ed.
Madison County Schools
Huntsville, AL

Publishing Credits

Conni Medina, M.A.Ed., *Managing Editor*
Lee Aucoin, *Creative Director*
Torrey Maloof, *Editor*
Lexa Hoang, *Designer*
Stephanie Reid, *Photo Editor*
Rachelle Cracchiolo, M.S.Ed., *Publisher*

Image Credits: Cover, p.1 Maria Pavlova/Getty Images; p.4 Alaska Stock/Alamy; p.18 Blend Images/Alamy; p.2 Cultura Creative/Alamy; p.24 SCPhotos/Alamy; p.2 comptine/iStockphoto; p.5 jose1983/iStockphoto; p.11 stevegeer/iStockphoto; pp.6, 8,10, 12 Stephanie Reid; p.19 Teacher Created Materials; All other images from Shutterstock.

Teacher Created Materials
5301 Oceanus Drive
Huntington Beach, CA 92649-1030
http://www.tcmpub.com

ISBN 978-1-4333-7346-6